THE BELOVED
COMMUNITY

Also by Patricia Spears Jones

A Lucent Fire: New and Selected Poems
Painkiller
THINK: Poems for Aretha Franklin's Inauguration Day Hat, editor
Femme du Monde
The Weather That Kills
Ordinary Women: An Anthology of New York City Women, editor

THE BELOVED COMMUNITY

Patricia Spears Jones

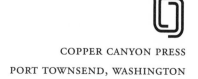

COPPER CANYON PRESS

PORT TOWNSEND, WASHINGTON

Cover artwork: Stanley Whitney, *The Freedom We Fight For,* 2022. Oil on linen, 80 × 80 inches (203.2 × 203.2 cm). © Stanley Whitney. Photo: Rob McKeever. Courtesy Gagosian.

Copper Canyon Press is in residence at Fort Worden State Park in Port Townsend, Washington, under the auspices of Centrum. Centrum is a gathering place for artists and creative thinkers from around the world, students of all ages and backgrounds, and audiences seeking extraordinary cultural enrichment.

LIBRARY OF CONGRESS CATALOGING-IN-PUBLICATION DATA
Names: Jones, Patricia Spears, 1955- author.
Title: The beloved community / Patricia Spears Jones.
Description: Port Townsend, Washington : Copper Canyon Press, [2023] | Summary: "A collection of poems by Patricia Spears Jones"— Provided by publisher.
Identifiers: LCCN 2023015229 (print) | LCCN 2023015230 (ebook) | ISBN 9781556596667 (paperback) | ISBN 9781619322820 (epub)
Subjects: LCGFT: Poetry.
Classification: LCC PS3569.P4176 B45 2023 (print) | LCC PS3569.P4176 (ebook) | DDC 811/.54—dc23/eng/20230330
LC record available at https://lccn.loc.gov/2023015229
LC ebook record available at https://lccn.loc.gov/2023015230

9 8 7 6 5 4 3 2 FIRST PRINTING

COPPER CANYON PRESS
Post Office Box 271
Port Townsend, Washington 98368
www.coppercanyonpress.org

To my peers, who have shown great faith in art, poetry, and community.

Someone has walked this way before
All the world's music in her hands
Under the starlight
That she wished
Could lead away to freedom

LORENZO THOMAS, "DISCOVERING AMERICA AGAIN"

CONTENTS

Two

THE BELOVED
COMMUNITY

*The female worker was also one of the last groups to leave
the South. (1941)*
The female workers were the last to arrive north. (1993)

CAPTIONS BY JACOB LAWRENCE

Lave

Where is the lavender, the purple scent
That says the world is fresh and ready to receive
The woman who walks into whatever room
She walks into. What room will she enter?

How will the female worker smell? Lemon, mint,
Roses crushed for homemade soap. No place
Here for the boiling recipe. There is no room.

And her extra money, how will she make it?
Who will she *do* for? How will she get there?
Will she find her old friends, her lovers?
She is lonely.

The artist says in Panel 57 that the female worker
(not Negro, not migrant) *is the last group* to leave the South.

One woman is her own group?
Was she ready to leave or was she
Left behind? Caring for: baby, grandfather,
Brother, sister, cousin, an elderly aunt?
Was her garden where the family sought nurture?
Were her skills at picking cotton so great
The bosses did all they could to keep her.
Was there a fourth child, not wished for?
Do her skills at baking, barter, cooking,
Cleaning, farming, soap making
Create a one-woman group?

The series narrates whole communities departing
Excited, wary, desperate, adventurous.

3

Much about the South is unseen or not shown—
The painter understands the usefulness of obscenity
Lynching
Hunger
The crops failing (boll weevil, boll weevil)

And so, we see the cotton ball
But not the bleeding hands that pick.
We see the rope dangling.
We see the meagre rations of meat
And bread. And the table set—no plenty.

Is this the start of a woman's true blues?
The men go ahead/The women stay behind, and everyone is lonely?

In many of the paintings' planes, she is not seen
preparing the meals, cleaning, sewing, packing
Clothes to last for as long as they can last in the
Distant cities of Chicago, Pittsburgh, Detroit.
She is not seen crying at the preacher's table
Or burying her head into the broad chest of the man
Who gets up before sunrise to make it to the station
Ticket in hand.

The men knew the hardships ahead; others were ignorant
Enough to believe the stories of plenty of work, plenty of
Food, plenty of shelter. All wanted a way out of
Dixie on a very bad day. Wanted out of stuck.

Women might want to believe in these stories—tall tales
But too many unwelcome hands, tongues, penises had found
Their bodies much too easily. A white man's promise
Of a better life up past the Mason-Dixon Line is some *thing*
to believe when fish fly on Friday and hogs dance a reel.

She will leave for the north and go to the cities.
She will find the church where her bible meets the preacher's
Holy hollering and the music sounds as sweet
As in the backwoods.
She will see the kind of dresses she wanted to make
From the Butterick patterns at the notions counter.

The same counter where she finds the yellow ribbons
That tie the braids of the young girl in Panel 21
who arrived early to get on the train.
Going North.

Is this the start of another woman's blues
To journey north and find the men mired?
To journey north and find her skills unknown?
To journey north and discover an even greater loneliness?

The female worker gets that ticket and joins that
Motion forward—the many shoulders, legs,
hands stretched across the paintings' frames counting
The rails away away away from Dixie Land.

Head bowed, holding an orange dolly,
The laundress is charged with purgation,
Removing the dust and dirt and stains of city living
The marks of many sins: sex, drink, the opium den.

These swirling oblong colors rest
Beneath her gaze as if she has the power
To make this job seem better than
Picking cotton or hog butchering or taking
In washing for the old Gentleman
Who pinches her breasts for that extra
Nickel.

Last to arrive north.
But first to see the way home/to make a home.
Puts her skillets on the hot plate; shelves her mason jars
Full of peach preserves, pickles, tastes of home.
Chenille spreads on the lumpy mattresses
The Chicago Defender on a kitchen table.
Biscuits rising before sunrise.
Greens found in a market run by Italians.

She stands in this painting
A cruciform of desire
In a center of beauty
Dressed in white, the orange stick

Her cudgel, her sword. The laundry
Her step on that ladder to the future.

A migrant from the back of the bottom
Or a town just big enough for the railroad to notice
Gone to the city and its bitter possibilities so that
Church is hearthstone and eau de cologne—
Lavender, roses, vanilla, hints of   a necessity.

ONE

Someone has walked this way before

LORENZO THOMAS, "DISCOVERING AMERICA AGAIN"

Morning Glory

Sunlight softens   helicopters hover
Skies above Brooklyn   Presidential
Visit, murder investigation, matters little.
Noise in the skies, noise on the ground.

You should prune the morning glories
I tell my elderly neighbor.
She refuses. She likes the way the vine has
Curled around her fence with a ferocity
That cannot be so easily cut back. I get that.

Wildness is rare on a Brooklyn city block,
Old roses return late May as if to say, ha! you
Think we do not know the season? Squirrels
Roam the bricks of buildings, while the gleaners
Fight with raccoons for the spoils of left-out trash.

Huge green leaves for plants with names
Unknown to me sparkle on mornings bright
And dead tree leaves demand constant sweeping away.

The tabby is big, old, and tired—too many kittens
Not enough food—these are ungenerous cat lovers.

Neighbors greet each other and shake their heads
At the young men and women, mostly, but not
All Whitefolk running running—or their faces
Drowning in a pool of handheld devices.

You almost wish they smoked or cursed
Had personality—but they run and run and run
Thus, the joy of this vibrant morning-glory vine
Rooted in her garden's disarray—happily dominating.

Oh, morning glory—purple, green
Leaves plump as Italian cookies, blossom
Your hearty display for all to see, hold your
Vine's haven on Macon Street. Only

Winter, harsh winter will take your vines
Back to the ground   your wildness calmed.

All my real live love interests are dead
They are artists & Latino & dead

Oh, That Brazilian Guy

Did I ever see Hélio—walking some part of
East Village, curly headed and densely
Packed with art and drugs and death's
Constant shadow. Was he on the corner of
Avenue B and 10th Street drinking beer
And ogling the pretty Puerto Rican girls.
Was he ogling me?

Or was he living in an abandoned warehouse
Holding on to his pencil, pen, brush on paper, cardboard,
Found trash or garment-district fabric off-loaded by a gang
Out of the projects whisking splatter of heroin (lost income)
Dropped dangling from a cup of bitch's brew

Oh, how to speculate this mad Hendrix-loving
Artist's movements in El Barrio, Loisaida, or was he
Uptown, Spanish Harlem or on the West Side, Greenwich
Village, hanging with the drag queens early a.m. everybody
Tired from the bars, the piers, the crumbling edifices
Circa late '60s, early '70s Nueva York, Nueva York?

He was on a wild ride the weed his stash the dazzled dreams
of men who had
Survived torture military repression a bad economy
Yet learned to take acid trips one day at a time.

Oh, the love affairs we have with the myth
Oh, the what-ifs and that drug paraphernalia
Oh, night seeker, ill named, moon winds
Your direction home?

Thus is created this mixed-up third whirl, loud music, your lips
Dry from screaming in January wind—something mighty Hendrix

Sun lack
On a back meant for napping midday, heat exhausted.

Thus, the making of a hammock a thing of beauty,
Backlit by the gallerist
While duct tape coiled the rafters of some street-legal post
Fly-fishing flies
Pretended bait. Tight pants dropped here and there.
As thriving masquerade—of the handsome Brazilian
Who could have been the best *badnews* boyfriend ever.

Poverty

Is a broken tooth
No smile—

Is bone poorly reset
Weak limbs, medicos various.

The fear of speaking unless spoken to

Fine translation skills—
A dollar means
A late bus is

An opportunity falters
At the site of   cracked tooth

Who are you
Is really
Why did you come here?

American geology is harrowing
An unlikely loveliness grows
In cracks beside crack houses

Trophic Cascade

The city is as good a place to learn about the ecology of fear
As any quadrant in the mountains of Wyoming or Colorado

You can see how people shift their talk-voices higher or lower
When the young bloods fall in formation—alphas up front
Wannabees in the rear. Elbows jut and feet seem bigger—

Air Jordans, Air America, Air apparent, Air regardless

Thus, the terms *streetwise* or *smart-ass* or *alert* and *do not
Linger.* Where the streetlights go dark and there is no
                    (streetlights one word)

Moon to speak about or ignore. As if waves mean nothing
And of course, waves mean nothing.

Trophic cascade *refers to the movement of energy through the
community food web when predators are removed (or when they
return).*

CRISTINA EISENBERG, *THE WOLF'S TOOTH*

Lee Breuer dies and I clean my stove top

Clove calls me at 10 a.m. or so. She lives in California.
Her voice is rumbling. Sad volume. You should know
That Lee is in hospice. I did not know that Lee is in hospice.
She says she had time to sit and talk to her father.
Her brothers had time to sit and talk to their father.
What a Luxury. A break from distance placed between
The living and the dying, those pandemic-built walls,
But this is cancer. This is organ failure. This is old age.
This dying. Thus, the family makes traditional gestures
For an unconventional man. His muses living and dead
Most likely shout him quiet. And the fast-talking man
Is mute.
Who sparks your path is always a factor of fortune.
Good fortune, and light remains lit no matter the brambles.
Bad, and all is shadow and stumble and loss. Oh, fortune
For me was good, and I clean my stove top. The old
Stove's top has age stains and boiling-over pots, stories
And memories of landing feetfirst in the muck of art making.
Every memory a pebble, stone, rock of learning. Lions
Die in quiet or in roar. Lions die. That light moves
To one more and one more and more—pilot light.
Yes, pilot light.

Saturnine

We cannot feel microbes in the palms of our hands
or hear nanoseconds—we can see the laser slice wind. But
how it shaves beards remains mysterious.

This talk of science & biologicals & viral crowns
makes old mean men crawl into bolls of cotton
waiting to be plucked at some point
by cadaver slaves humming Tin Pan Alley tunes.

What's a pandemic
but one more mortality wake-up call? Tongue dulled by wine salted
and cabbage stews happily forgotten. Buffed shoes shining, not worn.
No more the perfect Windsor Knot because the definition for *knot*
has swerved from necks to bandages.

If ever we could color the subatomic particles and smash them up
would they look like a Ken Tisa Quarantine Drawing—how that
could brighten the feet step-by-step in August air. The summer

feels like a heavy cough that starts in the chest, lingers
until it exhausts patience and runs up through the throat
out into the embracing air carrying all manner of microbes, some

of which or what could possibly infect a city or laugh pyrotechnic
4 a.m. along with feral snarls and cheap guns shooting, poor man
falls—
mercy walks down a different block.

Fortune's Wheel

Fortune's wheel turns with thunder's sway
I'm seventeen, homeless, can you help me
With a dollar

Seventeen, dollar
Homeless, dollar
Help me, dollar
The mighty wheel rumbles beneath
Streets paved with grime and magic

Heard, seen, but not helped
Seventeen grumbles
Got to get off this train

The city pitiless, the city cashless
The wheel's roaring
Doll smashing, dog lashing, lights limn
Avenues paved with magic and time.

Walking on Avenue A on the Tompkins Square Park Side

We are walking Sandra Payne and me on an unpeopled Avenue A.
It is dark but too dark and even in the daytime, it's dark on Avenue A.
We walk on the sidewalk on the Tompkins Square Park side, no dogs,
We see Steve Cannon driving a sedan. He rolls down his window
Want a ride? Sandra waves no, but I say hey he may be going farther,
So, we go over to where he is parking his car. It's 7th Street—he parallel parks
On Avenue A & 7th Street so the garageman can check his car.
This is the unblind Steve, the un-glasses Steve, his eyes bright brown
but what is strange is his hair. He has too much straight black hair.
It's a wig, a sort of bad Beatles cut with bangs. Steve Cannon with bangs.
He's smiling but the hair, it's post chemo wig hair. It's the worst haircut
you've ever had and must cover it up wig hair. Steve had that New Orleans
Mess With Me hair. The wig is a rebuke of all that New Orleans flare.
Steve smiles, patient with the garageman. His ride is a Volvo?
It's roomy and safe and he salutes Sandra and me and we salute him back.

New Orleans BOP

Falsetto hits those high notes "On the Radio,"
Donna Summer celebrated. Remember, he wore
A red jumpsuit with sequins in distinctive pattern.
A one-hit wonder of a man doing an early set
For old friends in his bar, typically Black—
The red banquettes, the loop the loop smoke
From desolate cigarettes. Tom Dent was alive.

The lights are never bright, this is not Broadway.

The red jumpsuit, the heavy, permed hair—
James Brown's late-'70s do exaggerated
How the material stretches, his voice a token
Of feminine energy—and yet the swagger
Is masculine—a '70s idea of gender-shifting
Ambivalence on display. Tom Dent gently gossips.
Recollection, Tremé, under a shaking superhighway
New Orleans, late '70s. Tom Dent is dead.

The lights are never bright, this is not Broadway.

Tom Dent is dead. Memory tremors—Tremé, New Orleans,
and Donna Summer is "on the radio" falsetto in a dusky place
his red, sparkling jumpsuit asks us to see the singer
Feminized and so we do. Song over and voice drops
As fast as blood or semen spilled, oh so quickly
Across the pleasure canals of this water-surrounded city.

The lights are never bright, this is not Broadway.

Leontyne Price sings "Pace, pace, mio Dio"

Peace, peace my God
Peace, peace my God—the piece that fell there
Here, the piece that falls and keeps falling
My God—we need peace, peace

The crows seek shelter
Perch there
Perch here
Perch up near the lamplight line
Sidewalks splattered with crow shit
It's all hit and never miss—the crows laugh
Loudly. They caw and caw as in a cartoon.

Then swoop up again searching for
A line of wire strong enough to handle gossip.
Perch here
Perch there

A noisy line of brassy birds
Ready to eat up all the leftovers—heck,
The pigeons refuse this massive waste.
Species specialization or just the luck of the draw.
Claws when needed for the rescue or respite.

Peace, peace dear God.
The Soprano sings her plea.
She wants calm, a serenity
Not the violent destiny that opera
Brings to all women—the dagger,
The strangled neck. Peace, peace
My God, why the dagger, the poison,
The strangled neck—when did art
Become the home of murderers?

The crows know that humans are malicious
And wasteful. They calculate the many droppings
We dispose of: meat, bread, dead dead vegetables.

20

They can taste what they want, but what sickens us
Sickens them.

Pace, pace, mio Dio
Pace, pace, mio Dio
Peace, peace, my God.

Purgatorio—divine comedy—again

Return again to Canto VI, the *Purgatorio,* and the gambler
Leaves. Her garment of sadness wraps her roughly. Lost
Stars rise and fall as do her tears—this is not an exact

Translation. Book opens to that image reoccurring a
Decade since first read, understood, *dolente,* what
Sadness held in those syllables mouthed centuries

Ago. The poet in exile. The in-between Heaven &
Hell. Interstices. Adrienne Rich wrote about these
In-betweens. Where women's live-action agency

Often falls—heaven and hell. In time and out. We
Talk loudly now yet are dismissed again by a ritual
Deafness of leaders: political, cultural, spiritual.

Our garments wrap us. But we wear our shoes
We sing our blues. Have hands strong enough to throw
One more set of dice, drink that cup of wine—may the splatter

Stain the chummy *gente* who curse our courage.
The blood dribbles down their sagging chests.

Something's in the air

Boys keep running into and out of the Deli,
Pointing and laughing, not a loud laughter but the muffled
Conspiring kind—something's in the air, the heat, July,
The boys' energized gestures, even the old men
Join them and then as I walk through the portal
A fat Black woman, her breasts the size of small melons,
walks up Washington Avenue, for once, an apt analogy.
She is bristling, her speech barely audible, her half-
Nakedness is as loud as the high temperature.
Where did she come from, where is she going?
Her large feet march slowly toward Lincoln Place.
The boys are yelling—some call her crazy
But not one calls her bitch,
Her bare breasts, her nappy head, her shoeless feet
Her raging sweat—she is this day's mean heat.
She's a walking excavation of hurt. The boys
Bike away, amplifying the atmosphere with mute
Gestures, their laughter. Again, the naming
As she moves shirtless and shoeless, sweat screaming.
We know some of her anger. We see her shamelessness.
Some call her crazy. Some gesture the shape of her breasts.
But no one, not one boy, calls her bitch.

Betye Saar's *Mystic Chart for an Unemployed Sorceress*

My runes are in ruins, little laughter here for my sarcasm
What to do, this chart confuses, conflates moon, which phase
And honey, local or from some exotic shore and what of money
My savings stuffed beneath deflating mattress. Each cold

Day warns me that my résumé is unworthy. Who will hire me
Now that my spells are so easily broken, my warnings useless

It is a wonder that I worked as long as I did. Incantations
Memorized and recipes for spells written in an ink too pale
for visibility—each item sourced, the medicine worked and then

It did not. Was it the well of stories drying up. The fish scales
Stinking the kitchen table. The cat wandering away, while
Spiders spread their cosmic maps unreadable to all but
The other spiders. They cheer me. Again, I read the signs

Oh, how the signs obscure true knowledge and I am blazed
In this dark room, hungry, cold, and searching   who is this thief
And why has she cast this curse. What must I do to bring
Runes from my parched throat, medicine back to my pockets.

Mermaid and Surf

Looking at the modest buildings on Mermaid Avenue
The signs chatter English/Spanish/sort of Chinese
As the bright sun's cracked rays splash walls and windows
You see that Mermaid is where locals go to pray at a Shrine
offering solace & recovery, buy mangos & apples & chicken
or get their hair done by African women all the way from Timbuktu
Surf Avenue is the boundary between neighborhood
and fun seekers' noise & trophies & candy, beaches, bikinis & beer
There we spy the Secret Psychic's Shack. She's not there to offer
Solace in the name of a soulmate desired, but she does not need
to tell us about death, which is everywhere. Hear it in the shouts of
riders from the top of looping rides, in the Atlantic's dark waves
& the cut flesh and burned hands of the fry cooks come for
The American dream, but lately riding the night's angry mares.

First and last nights in Virginia, January and May 2020

First night in Virginia, we stop at a CVS, late, the store is vast & sorry.
The lone clerk slow wipes a counter. She slumps, sags, all that worry
in her spills onto the counter's hard plastic top. I gather items & wait
for her suddenly cheerful acknowledgment. It seems as if fate has
made this place a symbol of American want—everything in this place
seems cheap except the products for sale. The lighting, the railings, that
counter. This is replicated in Walmart, Walgreens, only the Dollar Store
does not pretend to be anything other than a repository of things you
need and things you don't. The clerks are not well paid & at night left
to fend for themselves in this plastic vastness. On my last visit, the clerk
stands behind a cheap plastic protector. More symbol than reality.
She wears her mask and behind it smiles—she has a job & that's good,
but this is yet another display & she's expendable. We all are.

Morning Song

You wake up to the phrase "salt lick"
You realize you know not one thing
About salt licks—you know salt
And lick but together? How does
The salt lick lick salt?

You know you are moving
To the land of word games
Or musical instruments
Unstrung, battered—too much play

Each day the gleaners walk sidewalks
In search of bottles. They separate
Already separated bags to find precious
Glass—that is plastic. They hate the cans

They know the places where beer
Overwhelms soda, where huge milk
Cartons say children, many children
Live here. They do not whistle when they

Work. They do not lick sweat
Off tired arms. They go about
The business of poverty with grace
And noise. Early morning dragging
The weight of others' waste.

Answer This

O Oracle where are the jewels? thief—
you drew the light from sapphires and
lifted the pearl's sheen.
How can you prophesy? How can you declaim
when we're down in the day's dirt
licking our self-made wounds to dust?
O Oracle, we owe you nothing but
the question, always, always the question.

COLLABORATION WITH ADA LIMÓN

Lytic, or how not to see The Strawberry Moon

The poet had too much to drink and so forgive her this lyric spelled *lytic*.
Lytic are these stars in full array above the myriad evergreens oh how
They light the austere lawns of French estates but why French estates
In the *Sierra Nevadas*? Eyes leap over peaks of these massive hills
Searching for clarity, but tongue sings gardens & the genesis of stories.

Consider the spirit of summer solstice in gratitude and perplexity.
The moon cannot be seen. The sun refuses to set with time enough
For the poet to see the large, red, promised moon, the strawberry moon.
The poet is perplexed by this seemingly endless day light
The sun's refusal to surrender to night,

the mountains, these mountains are as drunk as the poet tonight—
the pollinating pine, the restless predators, and their prey like
the moon moving where the moon moves—dipping her raiment in red dye.

Sun and moon and creatures hunting across mountains—then barking dogs in
SUVs populating small segments of wide parking lots. The wind chimes cheer.

Who will tell us our stories? Who will want to hear about drunken poets?
The origin of "the strawberry moon"; how gardens blossom beneath these
Stars' intensity. Luminous. Light. Clarity, Clare. Clara, oh, poets nimble
work these bones. Be done unto terra and air. Tales composed in patterns
of flight and tusk, gold and rubies, pine trees and mountain lions.

Our songs start in exuberance and anxiety.
Spirits work our blood and in the night's darkening air.
Making bracelets of gemstones & animal bones
culled from blood oaths and rifle butts,
& tongues undone by drink and altitude.

Self-Portrait as *retratos de cosas locas y de locos* (stolen)

Shall we have cocktails while slipping about the
Edge of Catastrophe—gin and tonic for summer
Whiskey sour for fall. All is not well, yet sun
Illumines green-leafed trees, soon bare   soon bare

Our eyes prowl fence edges for morning-glory vines
Our ears gallop from the booming bass of pumped-up cars
Our legs move as swiftly as a catamaran in dock
We mock the heavens with calls for Paradise Now.

Artist perambulating the shadowed alleys of downtown Manhattan
Memories of dream dulled in punk and rock clubs' filthy bathrooms
How much of what was is still now in the body in the bones of the body
Calcium loss   teeth loose   wrist smaller so all bracelets   jangle

Lips call repeatedly a song whose words are traces of tenderness
Yet sung too softly, as if only whispers could make the world hear.

Dancer

The man with the black feather tattoo pares this space
Between fantasy and the memory of a man's carved
Torso, designed for stroking and celebration.

Today the sun's brightness is like that lover's kiss,
Wonderful in the present and greater in memory

A memory that brings me back to that black feather's
Flutter. Stars dazzle in some other part of this world
Where the sun has set and the moon illuminates
Swans diving   into   voluminous waters.

Lipstick Considered

Aah to have a blossom colored by lipstick—nature
Saluted and mutated by chemistry.

Elizabeth Taylor lipstick bloom, poet says
But which Elizabeth Taylor lipstick—the lush reds hints
In those brightly lit black-and-white movies—say *Father of the Bride,*
Or the soft blush fake-innocent pink from *BUtterfield 8*
Marking that mirror NOT FOR SALE.

And these blooms in the Arizona desert
Angling toward or away from the sun's rays
Scars vast regions of America's south & west.
We can only speculate
how blossoms bless their beauty or curse it.

How they bless this blush of red, this smear of pink
The lips once generous with flesh, now less so.
But the pot of color is discovered
That almost imitates those desert blooms
Their natural rouge. And the poet's movie star
Shimmers in the night sky near her plane
Venus—seen so easily   too far to touch.

Seraphim

Once a beauty, full-figured, beloved,
And then a fever, sweats, water vomited
Until the body gave out. And then,

Wings and lyres and a legion of other Angels.
Singing, dancing, flying about

But once a beauty remembers
Physical love and then its loss

Eternal life seems mundane
No conflict or need or desire

Thus, this Seraphim held melancholy
Gentle as a lull in a long conversation

But heaven allows only jubilance
Possibly the angel needed to return

Human: with feelings, tears, and laughter
Or find a way to shape the sadness into
A moment of beauty when the angel's wings
Spread and flight moves to breathing
Full of vision. There the angel's tears bond
with the visitor's fear, awe. It could be

a filmmaker's perambulating Berlin,
in search of a reason to consider
the spirit, those angels set
on top of monuments across the handsome city

And they love the lovers.
And one remains lovingly disinterested.

How dreams and death and a dearth
Of joy is visible. And wings spread
And wings fall. And the beloved becomes

A man who understands a woman's
Full figure. A man who fears fever.
A man who takes his lover in all
Her melancholy and lifts her up

And unto joy.

Siren Song

I have no metaphors today. All the analogies are taken.
No one is wise enough or kind enough or smart enough
To say what nobody wants to actually (should) say:
Sex is messy.
Humans hurt one another
Power shifts depending on who wants what more
And everybody knows how to blame.

There is no shame in owning the truth of one's ambition.
Or the topsy-turvy ways in which we switch on or off
What we think will get us what we want. He wants sex (maybe)
Or she wants sex (maybe) or both think that is what they should
Want and then he does something stupid or she acquiesces at
An inopportune moment or they find themselves at 3 a.m.
Waiting for 7 a.m. to come. That's the easy part. The dull
Date part.

It's the other uglier part that gets the headlines. The mad talk.
The guy who just happens to have hands in places where they
Received no invitation. The guy who thinks his girlfriend, his wife,
His daughter, his sister, his mother is a punching bag—oops, that
Metaphor. The guy who brings roses for bruises. The guy who
Calmly drives his car across the mother of his four children.
That guy. He is a menace to society and we all know it.
So how does he get away with doing this daily, hourly, by the minute
And why are all these roses stomped on?

In the grave are too many women who once had roses
For bruises. In offices, too many women who have
Had hands placed uninvited across around beneath
Their bodies. In homes, there are fathers who find
Incest the anecdote for the dreariness of their wives
Or maybe it's the romance of it all.

The romance of it all is done for.
But the guys are stealthy and intelligent.
It is not the backlash, but the proffered alliance.

The sweet tongue trying ever so hard to say
Just the right thing to make all the wariness
The necessary wariness go away. In Greek mythology
Sirens are female, but now the gender's
Changed. Women watch for the rocks
Be careful the talk and examine the heart
The unhoneyed tongue may be a new undoing.

Fire can take a long time to ignite.

Anne Boyer makes a new word

Bellehole
Beautiful hole
Sophisticated slit

Thus, Slut and words of ill effect on females
A trail of blasted curses leads ever on to that
Valley of prosperous anecdotes—you know
The one about and then the other one and
The one that won her that prize, a husband,
No, the house.

Bellehole. Artifice pulsates the poet, singes swifts
busy flying tree to tree—while their banner of shit
droops down the hole in the roof—dumbass song—
Oh, house collecting somebody's debt. Wet

With memories and a tornado of ideas
Blow the damn hole! Reinvent
The sweet scent of early puberty when
Lampposts threatened to descend upon
shouting men, humoring their hormones
But getting not one glimpse or touch
Of the poet's perfected new word: *bellehole.*
Beautiful hole.
Cracked earth shuffling roots and roofs
Los Angeles is its own topographical feast day.
As the virgin girls screaming in crumbling
Buildings. What night is this? Whose feast
Is worthy of this temper, these cries, the claims
Of jesters.

Bellehole
Beautiful hole
Sophisticated slit.

Hannah's Cigar Box (memory & invention)

You meet a woman who says I see WORDS on my forehead, and she
designs brassieres. Why not, this is New York City, East Third Street,
and other poets are sipping something and chatting and the woman who sees
WORDS on her forehead has a generous laughter and kind manner and
why not see WORDS on foreheads or arms or trees or the backs
of scratchy jackets of hustling bums all begging and laughing and drinking
and if not in the flophouses then in the Men's Shelter across the street
where day care children tell me the drunks are old and the younger ones,
addicts—already, they understand the distinctions and the dangers.
It's an East Village world and buildings are creaky and shaky with age and
sadness. Many poets mad and hungry roam about at 3 a.m. on their way to Dave's
Corner or some other dive or if lucky a bustling Cantonese restaurant where
the WORDS are visible as racewalking and foreheads covered in curled
bangs or scarves and the green tea's sharp smokiness tosses mist and
burrows dreams in liquid notions of ways to puzzle M. Duchamp's urinal or
J. Cornell's cosmic boxes—whole systems jeweled and shiny encased
and displayed so that movie stars can see within them and find directions to Venus
or Saturn or restlessly return to Earth, East Village, New York City
and myriad kosmic-stenciled cigar boxes.

Thanksgiving/Boston 2013

Half-moon growing into full
Young men circle the square of concrete
Words pinging the air
Half-moon growing into full

In a friend's house the books and paintings
Harmonize a life of comfort, full furnished
Marriage in all its abundant contradictions

Intimacy and acceptance—a door that may be
Shut when needed. Ornaments of sharing—cups,
plates, wineglasses. Good beer and better whiskey.

Where as the light falters in the underground
Men walk tracks with headlamps at full blast
Danger abides. Danger abides

And so the tabloids print the face of a child murderer
Or the Pope—anxiety abides. Anxiety abides

And then doves are released—Brooklyn's lungs
Exhaling. A father's weeping farewell. Brings us
Their watchful generosity.
The beauty of their chatter.
The matter of their charity.

We have what we have. And each of us has lost
Someone dear—a child, a parent, a friend, a lover.
Over decades of growing into fullness, our years become that
Precarious blossom that falls onto earth and decays.

The Beloved Community

The Bangladeshi man walks slowly, so slowly
I know he is ill. He shuffles a broom about
The laundromat, then sits in front of the largest dryer.
Then a Latina comes in frantic pointing at the flier posted
on the laundromat's window.

"What happened?" she asks.
The attendant says—"She died."

"But when, how?"

"Two weeks ago. Two weeks," he says.
He knows only this. Dead, two weeks.

The Memorial is for later in the day, in a place
Far from Halsey. The flier's crisp image of a Black woman's face
Smiling, young looking, but she was not young. "Two weeks."

La señora shakes her head, her purple-streaked
Hair tamed by her sadness.

"She always said hello. She was always smiling."
She says this to me. I nod and try to smile with her memory.
She looks once again at the image, black and white, utilitarian
On the glass surface. Then walks out onto the sidewalk
Undone by new grief.

Poet

Please do not believe my beauty
Do not trust my love.

HSI MUREN, "AN ARTISTE" FROM *ACROSS THE DARKNESS*
OF THE RIVER

The poet is Mongol. A translator follows her heart
Once broken, and yet she sings in a way that makes
Her broken heart   my broken heart.

She is in exile. The mountains are now ruled by China
And her culture is assaulted daily—buildings blasted
Children made to learn Mandarin. This is all too familiar:
The ways of Empire, very old ones; very new ones.

But these are poems of love and poems of loss.
The lover's inconstancy is all too familiar.
Her laments are tender, then angry—there are many
Storms in her poems. They rise from the mountains
From the sea, from the rivers inside her veins.
They rise up.

And oceans far from her a woman reads her words
And quickly says, "Sister, I have been there." His hands
Holding mine. Gone. His lips no longer touch mine.

And yet, the yellow roses, the birthday kisses,
Our shared embrace of *deep-down* Chicago blues,
Those conversations knee-deep in a dream of
Dark loving. Tremble my heart.

And so you stand in the shadows at a train station
Looking for the moment your love steps off his train.
He is not alone and you will not be happy. The storms
Throb the streets of Taipei and scatter rose petals
Across the sidewalks and streets of Brooklyn.

41

TWO

Within their eyes before they too must look away.
At dawn, when the first buses leave, their great wipers arc
Like women bending through smoke

to burdens, singing terror, singing pity.

LYNDA HULL, "LOVE SONG DURING RIOT
WITH MANY VOICES"

Saturday Brooklyn, July 17, 2017

Soprano intones tears
Of rhymes, rhythm building
Ballad at breakfast

Cold rains returning
Brooklyn is green as the grass
In Lorca's fingers

Feet stroke carpet
Diva laughs, the camera clicks
Red shoes to the side

Poet's desk a mess
Notebooks, pens, invoices, clips
Rock-steady fire escape

an American haze

"Of thunderclouds, cracks and volunteers"
Trumpeter lilies argue the loudest scents—you could wrap
a fiesta with that smell

and when done, you will know you're at a funeral parlor
and tears are falling   falling

stars brighten dancing figures—the ones that Jasper Johns
remixes, O elderly DJ—got that pepper in his pocket

who knows these people in the desert: volunteers
come with food & water left for *desperados*—the menwomenchildren
stumbling into an American haze

they too, these volunteers, are illegal, told to leave
the desert un-footprinted even as the menwomenchildren
mark the earth calling on insects, birds, and beasts to follow
to gather   to take what is left of the stumbled bodies

The border between good and evil can be porous
Or hard as steel or an ideology of hatred—the country
Is full of ideologues and the border cracks.

Cousins

What genes we carry this making of Americans
The strands and strains of clashing clans/dishonored kinfolk
Dahomey meets Wales meets Cherokee Nation consider
A gentle shade of brown slant of eye the high planes
Of cheekbones or a lightness of skin tone—a troubling
And doubling of the tribal flourishing
Of course, some passed strange across these strata desperate

How the ploys undertaken denying birthrights, human rights
Civil rights succeeded or failed is the story we tell one way
Others tell it another way—truth is malleable like clay or
Corn and water. Or is left at the hanging tree—victims'
Dried blood borders the sad tree's root system. And cousins
Swear and swerve away from the traces of kin picked clean

By vultures. Kin cut names from their tongues, burn names
In the woodstove, throw names into the river. Forget the
Strands that link them blue eyed and blond back to Africa.
Generations give "no never mind" as the tumult of changes
Rumbles around them. Yet there is always one who keeps
The shame or the blame near to her mind's measure

Deathbed confessions or attics' messy furnishings/diaries
Unlocked and threads of hair touched again—who was kissed
Here and when? Who grabbed the girl and made her pregnant?
Who walked away when her father was lynched? Who snatched
Whose land? Who took it back? Those bright greetings

On Sunday mornings—Pastor to Pastor—congregation to
Congregation singing the same hymns but in different measures
How these cousins many times removed walk away from
One another. Full of mystery. Full of fear.

The skin of the thing

The sea rivets memory
Recalling boat names, ship titles
Manifests handwritten or typed.
Holds forgetting: stowaways tossed,
Suicides unknown. Refugees' fabrics,
heirlooms, jewels removed.
---------------------------- This human cargo
Tongues in search of listening ears—
The sea is here, the sea is there, the sea

Flicks waves against a high cliff's edge
Fear shadows the divers' reckless notion
A useful trophic cascade—mammal
Bodies are made of water, but land walkers
can only live near water, not on it, not in it.
        The swimmers care little for such calculus, but the divers peer into
Depths where the floating nameless gather.

They dive.
Then return face up out of water
Names called.
Splendor located

But others may find the wrong equation
Their number's up—an American locution
As in Are you Okay?

And if you're not Okay
How is the query answered?
Or is it ignored like a snoring lover—
You make do.

What is done for memory, to memory—how the skin
We wear softens or toughens depending on weather
Or whether we are touched or rebuked.

What are we to make of dreams in which one
Lover enters the skin of the other—surrenders
All but skeleton. How would that work, would
The lovers be Okay

Or is such surrender, a diver's risk, the cliff's
Edge comprehensible, then more jagged,
More dangerous than first surmised—too late
For such odd splendor.

----------------------------- Too much, the lover cautions
My skin is my own, more than a surface. Can we
Abrade each other, exchange lines of derma
This dust of ourselves is enough to share.
Hold to the lace that knits your limbs together.
Leave such violence to fantasists.

How to value a dispersal of self, a body dissolved
In love or loathing. Witness the bemused reports of bloated
Bodies come back to land, unrecognizable, unfamiliar.
Skin the color of forgotten if not taken in portions
In the aquatic garden. As if useless even in unlit splendor.

Who watches the lovers' quarrels, hears the curses
Of reckless divers, who can touch the skin's surface
How wounded is the tongue that asks such questions?

What a surrender of all aspects of their sixth sense organ.
Manifests: ink visible   the many unnamed washed up, washed away?

Dolly Parton, Emmylou Harris, and Linda Ronstadt sing "Telling Me Lies"

1

Somehow love

Was always the danger. Love, lust, that white girl
On the run. And if perhaps somebody colored helped
Her

Then he was a dead man walking
A lynched man foretold.

What are we to make of Mildred Loving, née Jeter, recently deceased?
Her married name on the case striking down the last of America's
Anti-miscegenation laws

She got tired of seeing her wedding certificate compromised.
Her children bastard in seventeen states and the District of Columbia.

How her family fought for the ordinary tribute to companionship:
Marriage. What a married name means in a world where
A young woman rides the rails

And suddenly becomes the woman endangering the lives
Of seven men, a hundred men,

Not even a prize like Helen, just a hellion
Trying to get away from the men who cut her speech in half.

You don't know a man until you have to please him.

2

And if you're the dark girl, pretty and smiling
If you're the brown girl walking down the road

And if the blond boy who loves you wants to marry you
What could you do before 1964?

How many
Walked away from their mothers, sisters, cousins
Passed into another land, just to have an ordinary life

Where their name meant what they wanted it to be.
White people invented—better ones?

Some we know.
Some we don't.

3

This pretty melody spotlights rage.
How your voices mingle
The danger and lonely witness southern women
White and Black lived

Through changes large and small
Like the one that the Chief Justice's pen permitted
Marriage between people whose skins thrived a different hue.

On the death of Claribel Alegría, 1924–2018

On earth, she marked her days with rage & love
and fought the generals and their army of thieves
and torturers. Her pen was mighty, so also their
Arms. Death is the shadow twin, the one remaining
In the foothills, by the back door, in a convent, off
A mountainside.

And yet, a mother's breast awaits her infant's mouth.
A rooster crows and children gather what food there is
While bells ring across the foothills when the soldiers
Leave. A music of hope even as another child is buried
And a land mine erupts a few kilometers from hospital.

We live in a time of suffering in places of beauty
Where the water and air meet in mountains dark-soiled
Food grows effortlessly and so does greed.

We live in a time of suffering in places of beauty
Where yesterday's rebel is today's president
And greed cowers the hurt children who hunger
Not only for their mothers' milk but a safe place
Where peace storms the land with smiles
and the tender removal of all aspects of war

A phantasm of peace. A peace unlike the other Ones—
negotiated and then neglected, thus
Military rifles, handguns, machetes, bowie knives, unexploded land mines
All made so that peace will end and terror return

What you hear is the sea—the heavy waves come in
Go out. Stars pattern—Orion's belt, or is that his heel?
And then another woman of letters departs, will she
Step on Orion's heel?

Would she say, excuse me, I did not see your heel.
Would she try to hide her error as her celestial
Garments drag across the night sky. What if Orion

Could speak, and if he did, would he say, all the
Poets love my heel or my belt, you're not the first
To seek an anchor here.

Crying in Cassis for The Queen of Soul—Aretha Franklin dead at 76

The Queen of Soul breath gone on an August night
or was it early morning—near dawn
The Queen of Soul whose reign was challenged
By baby divas with scurrying voices—rose up
But they never got near to her throne. She was
Born a citizen of a nation that called brown people
Queens and dukes and earls and counts, but rarely
Citizen. Born citizen of a nation that found tongues
Loosened in the framed temples of justice, love,
And recognizable rage. God's people vilified
God's people saved in rhythm, rhyme, time
Kept better with the beating back of those who
Could not name the God they worshipped (Mammon)
Or offer succor to anyone not like themselves.
Voice travels across hearts' doors, which once opened
Could not be closed. Voice travels deep in the hippocampus.
Mocked and degraded, open up and hear these words

**THINK RESPECT TROUBLE LOVE RESPECT LOVE
THINK THINK THINK THINK THINK THINK LOVE**

French voices shout in the bright late afternoon—the
Mediterranean sparkles today. It will sparkle tomorrow
But the heavens, oh, they will sparkle like never before.
The Queen of Soul. The voice that marked and framed
A generation of citizens American, then global SOUL
In Dakar, Accra, Tunis, Johannesburg. SOUL in Marseille
Manchester, London, Paris, Berlin on the radio
In Cologne, Santiago, Tokyo, and Chiang Mai.
Her voice trails Memphis, St. Louis, Chicago, Detroit
Great Migration in chords and harmonies, melodies memorable
Choruses repeated. Trails of tenderness and terror.
Woman on the road. Body loved, betrayed, slapped about,
Salved with new kisses. Woman on the road.
Queen of the train tracks, bus routes, plane rides,

Car trips. The Great Migration's circles of motion
Moving in her voice, a legacy. Her star matters
Brightly as Mars so keen to be seen this annum.
Battle weary resting

For Geri Allen

She's sitting in the half-moon's cup
Earthly roads have led to this new geography
Planets and stars—dust returns.

Her hands besotted with this cosmic baby grand
Playing starlight and a vast blackness
Shifting with her tender tempos
Pacing the eternal—oh, darkling descant
Blackbirds and fireflies trace her
Unhearable
musings
In this evening's skies

Ghost Country

One friend stands in a stand of beeches.
Enshrouded in shadow, but the sunlight shimmers
Over the water, behind her. There are days when you know
You're in ghost country.

No howling winds or webs extending the geometry of corners.
It is a name sung on internet posts
It is the lot where once there were dances and now
Children in prams look up at parents and other big people.
They want out of the prams
They can feel feet dancing.
It is a lover's name come up in conversation
Never quite forgotten or forgiven
Or that splash of cold water on a cold morning.

Ghost Country is where inhabitants are
Memories and Expectations. Things traced
Elsewhere now here with you—synapse
After synapse. Assured of colors and lines long
Lines short—this web, the corners edged with frigidity—

Winter's sloshy tune. Draughts and coughs
And trees in a forest, well hidden, consecrated?

So that only explorers of the highest caliber
Who speak the believers' language
Can see in the traces of what is yet to come
Holding dear, holding close, these shadows.

Milk Ice

Driving through fog and storm's aftermath
milk ice on leaves. From what breasts
Comes this milk?

Swelling and tectonic shifts plunging the snow's
Volume until a villa is covered from first floor
To roof—thirty people left in an exquisite tomb.

All that white. No present magic, but shamans once
Roamed these peaks and danced the valleys
In fur and branches listening for those slow shifts

Before the milk ice radiant, and a crystalline
Water packs the peaks, the heaviest of breasts.

The plows plod a path away from danger, the road clear
Vehicles move sloth-like around the curves descending.

And we hum what could become   lullaby
Fogged drive, bursts of sun, then tree leaves
Heavy with milk ice, a day's nurture.

Celia Cruz   Snow angels

The Great Gatsby jazzed the sorrows
Of summers where the wealthy misspend
Their wealth. Making the novice president
An apt arbiter of a future dulled by greed.

Thus, the novel's hero dead by his rival's gun
Tells this harsh truth:
Love does not conquer. Lakes are for icing   over.

Diversions come as random as this afternoon's
Mumble of news and sorrows and iced lakes.
Ah, Celia Cruz's Cuban Spanish brightens
What is she saying and is it Spanish?

Outside children in puffy jackets and
Christmas scarves are lying on their backs
In the new snow that takes their bodies'
Offerings. There's laughter. As moms
And dads and cousins and friends remember
Their time in snow's embrace. Angels
These bodies become. Angels. Brought
Down to earth and printed in snow.

What proof have we of these mythical
Creatures. Do angels laugh? Do they wear
Puffy jackets and patterned scarves,

Do they, once returned upright, begin to
Ball snow into projectiles and smash
Their kin. Are they cursing this whiteness
Do they hear Celia Cruz's potent voice
Singing in Spanish or maybe it is not
Spanish, but another tongue—denser
Deeper, from a haven on this earth
That she hears on blue days when the
Snow falls and children stuff themselves
Into winter's heaviest fabrics.

Then they fall quickly or slowly into a crystalline heaven
Their winged arms and leaping feet caught
In the beat between sound and sorrow.

Fred Hampton Born This Day

On August 30, in a town named Summit,
did the weather harbor danger:
droughts, floods, tempests across the prairie?
Was the hospital close by or did the family drive miles
To offer up a newborn baby boy

Clotho began to spin on that day a Black boy
Who grows strong in body and mind.
Loving, athletic, disciplined, enraged
Engaged with all who were

Black. Black.
Black in a world tilted   White
White
White
On its head, this world where Whiteness makes easy

         the gift of guns and conspiracies for killing anyone
Black.
Black.
Black and enraged.

Was it his black knit peasant cap on top of carefully trimmed Afro
or those Marxist-Leninist phrases he used at rallies
For the people (resisters to oppressions, resisters to greed)
Of the people (poor) by the people (Black)
That determined the brevity of his days walking earth?
Was it the web he was weaving bringing in Whites, Latinos, Native Americans
With Blacks—a communion of poor, enraged and seeking new ways to open doors
To quality housing, economic stability, food and health care, a war's quick end?
Was it that call for revolution, meaning human rights, meaning the right to stand
On a corner and demand just treatment, a decent life?
How could human dignity be such a Threat
And yet

Atropos held her sharp knife that cuts
The loom's ultimate threads—played out in
a scene of a 90 bullets government-planned rampage
by the uniformed conspirators.

One cold, startling December dawn,
his pregnant partner awakened, then dragged away
saving their only son for future battles.

Atropos, who never weeps, shook her unruly hair
As sign of her immortal distress.

Thus 21 years of living Fred Hampton's face
Is the crushed newspaper print where truth departed
Into snowmelt gutters and garbage bins, streaked
With mud and blood—as if he died in a barn
Another creature come to slaughter in Chicago.

Officers and bureaucrats covered this preholiday mess with
A lackluster cover-up expressing their ordinary brutality.
Power has a way of drifting out of clenched hands.

The rest is American history in blood, blame, and curses. Fortune's wheel
A proper setup for murderous deeds by credentialed men, each badge
        dishonored.

Only 21 years the fates could allow the virtuous man, more lion
Than wolf. Purr to roar. Summer heated,
30 August,
genesis day at the Summit in the middle of America.
Black boy breathing & squiggling, flesh as possibility.

Clotho wants to
Smile
But is not allowed.

Adornment

Red cap
Red scarf
Red balloon

A phalanx of protesters
A quarrel of militia—off camera
geared up
Prepared to muster
The musk of daily incivility
A roar of past coincidences
Blood's smell
Men's bodies.

The red cap
Of their hearts
Salutes an October day
Plush beauty—
can you smell the apples—
this fact of harvest.

On the round globe
Claiming our hearts' desire
To live more than eighteen years
Or whatever year it was
The bullets
Took.

St. Louis, Hong Kong, Mexico City
Wherever the young demand
Their future
A boy stands
Wearing a red cap
In the rain
In the heat
Observing the phalanxes
Coming down from the high-rises
Up from the basements

Out of the dormitories
Into the street.

The Poem at Sea

The poem found itself at sea. Poet forages another poet's
vocabulary—her words might prise open poet's mind-
locked chambers, reveal the posture of jellyfish.
Oh, this search for a key to closed chambers—
Ah, wavy words ripple and undulate, one poet's gift
To the other. The rigidity of imagery laps against a body's shore.

We are living lakes sloshing against other bodies.
Pardon, we say as spilling over—*chemo,* it is the word
Chemo, the poet marks

A boundary too often crossed
A procession of cells mutating
An attempted murder of mutating cells
The loss of parts beautiful: hair, eyebrows
The keepsake of an almost intact   body
That perfume of noxious sweats
Charts waves of tears, or salves hearts' muscle loss.

The poem is at sea. Observe
Distant from the harbor
Its journey toward massive cliffs
Far from this ravenous seagull
Eviscerating a pigeon on red rooftop

An ascent toward *abrasive* beauty.

"The pace of ferocity"

Night winds rush faces
Fabric or fur covers heads
Faces streaked with a ferocity of hatred.

Names called. Each one uglier.
Names called. Each one mis
Pro nounced. Mis represented

These world(s) we live in.
Feral howling the full wolf moon
Departing as grandly as the harvest moon
Arriving with harvest a deceptive harmony.

This lingering heaviness, these amazing feats.
Feasts in memory-made last days—marks of woe

Death-haunted man on side street,
Boy on sidewalk, young girl at door
Boy in a park. Boy in a park.
Marks of madness. Marks of woe.

Bearable a year of expected sadness
And then unexpected torments

Witness the *un* raveling of spirits
As the round earth spins.

Green Ribbons

Green ribbons flutter
& reside on lapels of women and some men
Green ribbons for the dark-skinned, skinny, chubby, light-
Complected boys and girls

Green ribbons for their safe return intact, smiling,
Scowling, howling, cursing, happy—oh, those dreams of happy
Endings. Everyone dreams of happy endings.

But Atlanta is where endings are ambiguous—tomorrow another day

Endings. Find the bloodied leg, the missing digits,
The raped vagina, the cutoff ear, the eyes left open for the birds
Or gently shut to mark tears. See no more. See no more.

Desperate are the mothers searching the wind for the sound of sneakers.
Desperate are the mothers who have not received that phone call.
Desperate are the mothers who gave their children money
To pick up milk at the corner store.

The cameras frame a tired woman's tired face. A tired man's tired face.
The abundantly furnished living room—cluttered but clean.
The microphones are probes into the innermost sadness of parents bereft.

The mayor intones EMERGENCY.

Police beat bushes. Beat up the older children.
Beat the time spent not worrying about dark-skinned, skinny, chubby,
Light-complected children. Beat themselves—why can't we catch this monster?
The kudzu, an immortal
Wraps the light poles and fences and drowns the air
With thick green madness. All summer long, the children

Walk into the green darkness and return as ghosts.
Ghosts scorch the green fields where they met the blasted heat of hatred.
Promise ended tomorrow is someone else's day.

Waving a kind of greeting to the newly Lost.

These ribbons impel a terrible keening each time they are pinned
To dresses, blouses, suit coats, jean jackets, green

Green ribbons. For the skinny, chubby, dark-skinned, light-complected
Boys and girls caught in the deep verdure of the city primeval.

Thus, these ghosts stalk the corner store and basketball courts
The Holiness Church where the minister sweats a flood of salvation.
They walk the halls outside the boys' & girls' lavatories.
They watch over the babies and shake their heads when

A mother smokes a pipe with no tobacco and a father is victim of
    a drive-by

They scorch the green fields with their ashy limbs running fast
They scour the distant wires loving the chatter of blackbirds. They
Sing sometimes, but only their parents can hear them. When they do,

They think red clay and graves.

Nia

It sounds better in Spanish, *precario*
Prettier. As if it isn't what it is, and there's that *o*

My, how will the rent get paid? The deadline
Met and who ghosted me first—valley lover
Or that other one.

Delicacy of skin. Quick steps, quick stops
And the direction is what?

There's no where there and the last shift
Is the one where tongues load a stack of sighs
Bridge tall and mythic.

This day and the next—volcanic shards
Roll toward the door, even if mountains
Are in the far distance—thousands of miles.

How the heart steadily beats as the sirens
Careen and angry men launch their best lives
Ever by taking so many others. It is a miracle

This heart steadily beating even as the next question
Threatens a late-spring storm, ground broken
By lightning—the raindrops' rhythmic patter

Honors percussionists—those that beat   beat
Their instrument with a purpose—Nia.
Knowing how one *off-beat* collapses the genesis
Augurs harsher storms—

Where the purpose becomes precarious.
Where death enters white armed, white throated,
Where the body drops like lightning on rain moist ground.

The Fifth of July, 2020

work like miasma   fount of boundless energy

un lifted   the weekly cross carrying   candles out

more tomorrow

               what of it
               when will it be

rockets

candles

fire

fire

candles

rockets

miasmic   beat beat beat the beat beat beat

sky lashed clouds   watery rage ready for release

rain thunder lightning summer's heartless mares   roaring skies

O say how we be   O say what we be

O say can we be   O say

Can we be

Free

Defiant

Fruit from one vine tangles with another
Making a mess of the intended harvest, yet
the lack of calculation is welcome

that accident that shifts bodies from shadows
into a locus of light midday bright & caustic
wounds unhealed newsreel cameras trap

this old & angry man in a bespoke suit lifting
white pages & refusing to read them, mumbles
unwelcome threats & thanks the nation

the nation kicks him out—finally defiant
after years of misrule, disruption, murder
and the choked-voice youth terrorized

he wants more blood on his hands so that
when he enters his version of paradise
all will be red.

LOOK BACK IN HATRED

There's a film poster with the line "don't look back in hatred"
On it the profile of a youngish Black man, distressed?

Who knows what the story is, but the title's admonition
Makes me ask: Why not look back in hatred?
There are situations, people who deserve ire.

They grab all the money, land, power.
They kill your sister or your mother.
They try to kill you.

They kill your brother or your father.
They try to kill you.

But maybe our youngish Black man has moved on.
Filled his heart with compassion. Learned to trust.
Come into the circle of kindness and wants
Never to leave. Good for him. But

What of the situation, the person, the time?
Where is justice? Who will stand accused?
And be judged? How will the law's slow reach
Find the killers, the exploiters, the vicious ones?

Don't look back in hatred. We desire Peace.
Harmony, yet, why not demand Justice?

I'd go see a movie called *Demanding Justice*.
I go see a movie about a real Django
Who joins up with John Brown's Antislavery
Brigade brandishing weapons and singing freedom.

A movie about a man whose heart has been whipped
Whose cries are heard by birds and crickets

A man whose hands have been broken
Oh, how he
Avenges the blasted hopes his body has

Carved in slow motion. In quick anger
In the tongues loosened only by drink
And fear. That man can stand with his hatred.
Mark its shape. Watch a ventriloquist

Tell the dummy's tale—bracing
Conjurer of numbers, locations, shifts in electricity

The man who looks back in hatred and sees
With gratitude the opportunity to smash
That dummy's blank
Face.

And the man's hand holds splinters from the touch
Of a wood so hard, it must be endangered.

Comedy with Flutes

Enough of this foolishness—caution gone
She opined
We need a comedy with flutes
Melody—the rise and fall of voices
Sweet or discordant, matters what to
Singing voice, the tune of it all.
These drums been beating for ages
And we can't decipher the signals—
Once the drum became a machine
The ghost in the skins was lost.

Give us the tickle, but not the slap
We need that cheer—the bombs making men rich
Depress the spirit, cauterize souls
weaken verve—we need
Our nerve back.

Rahsaan Roland Kirk return
With your many windy woods
Lift our souls up and out
Of this brutal banality.

There the not-so-young woman speaking
Sotto voce telling truth and when she does
The belly aches as you see her sitting on
The edge of wisdom. Playing her changes
Even as the drumbeats mechanize—the
Voice is our greatest magic. Listen for

The hard crunch fun of fighting back
Hear her lash the brute with verbs.

Speaking Sparks

Repeating news of police violence
beats back poetry.

The video feed fed well
digital drama loops,

myriad spirits trapped in pixels.
Their deaths tapestry the star sky.

On audio too many curses stuck
on FUCK FUCK.

When my daughter cries, "Mommy!
You told me not to say that!"
I reassure, "Honey,
my mouth is free.
In our house, we speak sparks
if we need fire.
Watch yourself
when you go out."

Here we are again,
weeping fears for breakfast.
For a year after the violence
I was scared to leave the house.
I carried mace, afraid
of my own clumsy hands.

Where did the "I" emerge,
frightened, housebound?

What does isolation mean?
Ice, location, danger from.

Our hands are shut in prayers.
Our hearts shut from fear.

But we have to go out.
Our words need air.

To survive. Sisters,
we mean to speak.

COLLABORATION WITH MARILYN KALLET

Notes

"Lave" was commissioned by the Museum of Modern Art for the Migration Series Poetry Suite accompanying *One-Way Ticket: Jacob Lawrence's Migration Series and Other Visions of the Great Movement North*. The exhibition opened in April 2015.

"Oh, That Brazilian Guy" is a fantasy dedicated to the Brazilian visual artist Hélio Oiticica (1937–1980) who lived in the East Village in the late '60s. He was a leading avant-garde artist, whose work is environmental, conceptual, witty, and sexy. He was queer.

"Lee Breuer dies and I clean my stove top" is for Lee Breuer (1937–2021), the theater director, playwright, and poet, and a cofounder of Mabou Mines, the renowned experimental theater company. My first gig in New York City was as prop mistress when the company performed at the Museum of Modern Art during the Marcel Duchamp retrospective.

"Saturnine" is dedicated to Karen Taylor.

"Walking on Avenue A on the Tompkins Square Park Side" is for Steve Cannon (1935–2019), novelist, publisher, cultural instigator, and founder of A Gathering of the Tribes.

"Self-Portrait as *retratos de cosas locas y de locos* (stolen)": The Spanish part of the title is from a work by Papo Colo, a Puerto Rican artist.

"Lipstick Considered" is dedicated to Pamela Uschuk.

"Hannah's Cigar Box (memory & invention)" is for Hannah Weiner (1928–1997), a poet who lived on East Third Street. She did see words, and her day job was designing brassieres.

"Thanksgiving/Boston 2013" is for Lynn Cadwallader and Richard Barran.

"Poet": Hsi Muren is a Mongolian poet based in Taiwan and is the author of *Across the Darkness of the River,* published by Green Integer.

"Saturday Brooklyn, July 17, 2017" is so named for the third anniversary of the killing of Eric Garner.

"an American haze": The poem's first line is adapted from a line in Brenda Hillman's "So, Bacteria Also Have Their Thunder."

"Cousins" is dedicated to Thulani Davis.

"Dolly Parton, Emmylou Harris, and Linda Ronstadt sing 'Telling Me Lies'": The poem references *Loving v. Virginia,* in which the Supreme Court struck down bans on interracial marriage, and the Scottsboro Boys, nine Black men accused of raping two white women in Alabama in 1931. The Scottsboro trial became a cause célèbre.

"Ghost Country" is dedicated to Kelle Groom.

"Milk Ice" is dedicated to David Rivard, whose Facebook post provided the phrase.

"Fred Hampton Born This Day" (August 30, 1948) is for the very young and highly effective chairman of The Black Panther Party in Chicago. The police brutally murdered him days before Christmas in 1969; he was only twenty-one years old.

"The Poem at Sea" is dedicated to Meena Alexander.

"Green Ribbons": Green ribbons were worn between 1979 and 1981, during the years of the Atlanta child murders when 29 Black children were killed. One suspect was arrested and charged, but not for those crimes. The murders remain unsolved.

"*Nia*" references the murder of Nia Wilson, a woman of color murdered by a white man in Oakland, July 2018.

"The Fifth of July, 2020" is dedicated to Anselm Berrigan.

"Defiant" was written in 2018 about Robert Mugabe (1924–2019), who was asked to resign from his "presidency" of Zimbabwe—on camera, he refused.

Acknowledgments

I want to thank the editors of the following publications, both print and online, for bringing many of the poems in *The Beloved Community* to readers:

About Place Journal: "New Orleans BOP"

The Academy of American Poets Poem-a-Day: "Dancer," "Defiant," "Saturnine," and "Self-Portrait as *retratos de cosas locas y de locos* (stolen)"

African Voices: "Celia Cruz   Snow angels"

The A-Line: A Journal of Progressive Thought: "*The skin of the thing*"

The Brooklyn Rail: "First and last nights in Virginia, January and May 2020," "Oh, That Brazilian Guy," "On the death of Claribel Alegría, 1924–2018," "Siren Song," and "Something's in the air"

The Cortland Review: "Hannah's Cigar Box (memory & invention)"

Cutthroat, A Journal of the Arts: "Purgatorio—divine comedy—again" and "Speaking Sparks"

LiVE MAG!: "Walking on Avenue A on the Tompkins Square Park Side"

Ms.: "Leontyne Price sings 'Pace, pace, mio Dio'"

The New Yorker: "Betye Saar's *Mystic Chart for an Unemployed Sorceress*," "*Nia*," and "Seraphim"

The Ocean State Review: "Poverty"

One: "The Poem at Sea"

Paterson Literary Review: "The Beloved Community" and "Lytic, or how not to see The Strawberry Moon"

Plume: "Anne Boyer makes a new word" and "Milk Ice"

Poetrybay: "Crying in Cassis for The Queen of Soul—Aretha Franklin dead at 76"

The Poetry Project website: "'The pace of ferocity'"

Prairie Schooner: "Fred Hampton Born This Day"

Recours au Poème: "Morning Song," French translation by Marilyne Bertoncini

Vox Populi: "an American haze"

"Answer This" is a collaboration with Ada Limón for the Center for Book Arts' Broadside Reading Series.

"Dolly Parton, Emmylou Harris, and Linda Ronstadt sing 'Telling Me Lies'" appeared in the chapbook *Stardust, landmines, and cartoons: Poems from 2006 to 2014.*

"For Geri Allen" appeared in *When Sugar Hill Was Sweet: Looking Back, Moving Forward,* the 2017 to 2018 program booklet for While We Are Still Here.

"Ghost Country" and "Green Ribbons" appeared in *Supplement,* the annual anthology of the Creative Writing Program and Kelly Writers House at the Center for Programs in Contemporary Writing (University of Pennsylvania).

"Lave" was commissioned by the Museum of Modern Art for the Migration Series Poetry Suite accompanying the exhibit *One-Way Ticket: Jacob Lawrence's Migration Series and Other Visions of the Great Movement North.*

"LOOK BACK IN HATRED" appeared in *Resisting Arrest: Poems to Stretch the Sky.*

"Lytic, or how not to see The Strawberry Moon" appeared in *Why to These Rocks: 50 Years of Poems from the Community of Writers.*

"Mermaid and Surf" was featured on the 92nd Street Y's #wordswelivein website and reprinted in *NYC from the Inside: NYC through the Eyes of the Poets Who Live Here.*

"Morning Song" appeared in *WORD: An Anthology by A Gathering of the Tribes* with a drawing by Yuko Otomo.

"Speaking Sparks" is a collaboration with Marilyn Kallet.

Without the generosity and critical recognition afforded me by the Jackson Poetry Prize sponsored by Poets & Writers, much of the work in this new collection might not have been made. I thank John and Susan Jackson for this generous gift and their significant support of contemporary American poets. The prize enabled me to attend the Robert Rauschenberg Residency in Captiva, Florida; BAU Institute at the Camargo Foundation in Cassis, France; and the Virginia Center for the Creative Arts. Gratitude to Hollins University for the 2020 Louis D. Rubin Jr. Writer-in-Residence that allowed me to develop the manuscript, teach wonderful students, and found me in Roanoke instead of Brooklyn during the first terrible months of the COVID-19 pandemic. The campus was a depopulated haven.

And finally, I want to thank some very good friends in and out of poetry. My poetry posse, who are great first readers/critics of new works: Margo Berdeshevsky, Angela Jackson, Maureen Owen, and Metta Sáma. Peter Covino, whose reading of the drafts of this collection gave me the courage to rethink, revise, and push forward, and Alice Notley, who read an early version. I am part of a diverse cultural community locally in New York City and around the world, who in different ways are voiced in this collection. Thanks to Tai Allen, Dawoud Bey, Alicia R. Blegen, Cheryl Boyce-Taylor, Michael Broder, Marie Brown, Lynn Cadwallader, Mary

Baine Campbell, Kyle Dacuyan, Beth Prussia Day, Marcella Durand, Janet Goldner, Deborah Wood Holton, Jason Hwang, Tyehimba Jess, Vincent Katz, Jeanne Larsen, Rachel Levitsky, Janice Lowe, John Edward McGrath, Atim Annette Oton, Nell Painter, Pamela Painter, Gregory Pardlo, Carol Paterson, Willie Perdomo, Jac'leen Smith, Patrice Tanaka, Karen Taylor, and Nancy H. Willard. And in spirit, the late artist Sandra Payne. I have two siblings who inspire and uplift me and love that I am a poet: Gwendolyn and William—we are all our Mother's pride.

This collection has been given extraordinary nurture by the Copper Canyon Press editorial staff: Thanks to Ashley E. Wynter, who is an amazing editor, and to Michael Wiegers for believing in *The Beloved Community*. And thanks to Stanley Whitney and the Gagosian for the vibrant cover art. The editors, the designers, the marketing team—everyone has been intensely supportive. I cannot say how much this means to me.

About the Author

Patricia Spears Jones is a poet, cultural activist, anthologist, educator, and recipient of the 2017 Jackson Poetry Prize. She is the author of five full-length poetry collections, including *The Beloved Community* (2023) and *A Lucent Fire: New and Selected Poems* (2015), as well as five chapbooks. Jones coedited the groundbreaking anthology *Ordinary Women: An Anthology of New York City Women* (1978) and *THINK: Poems for Aretha Franklin's Inauguration Day Hat* (2009). Her poems are widely anthologized, most notably in *Of Poetry and Protest: From Emmett Till to Trayvon Martin; BAX 2016: Best American Experimental Writing; WORD: An Anthology by A Gathering of Tribes; African American Poetry: 250 Years of Struggle & Song;* and *Angles of Ascent: A Norton Anthology of Contemporary African American Poetry.* Jones's poems are published in online and print journals such as *The New Yorker, Prairie Schooner, The Brooklyn Rail, Vox Populi, Paterson Literary Review,* and *Cutthroat, A Journal of the Arts.* Her essays, blog posts, colloquies, and interviews have been published in *Furious Flower: Seeding the Future of African American Poetry* and *The Whiskey of Our Discontent: Gwendolyn Brooks as Conscience and Change Agent.* They also appear in the print and online journals *The Black Scholar, BOMB, Mosaic, The Poetry Project Newsletter, The Rumpus, The Writer's Chronicle,* and *Harriet Books,* a Poetry Foundation blog, among others. Mabou Mines commissioned and produced two plays by Jones: *Mother* and *Song for New York: What Women Do While Men Sit Knitting.* Jones leads poetry workshops for the 92nd Street Y, The Work Room, Hugo House, Truro Center for the Arts at Castle Hill, and Brooklyn Poets, among others. She has received awards from the Foundation for Contemporary Arts, the Goethe Institute, the National Endowment for the Arts, and the New York Foundation for the Arts.

Poetry is vital to language and living. Since 1972, Copper Canyon Press has published extraordinary poetry from around the world to engage the imaginations and intellects of readers, writers, booksellers, librarians, teachers, students, and donors.

WE ARE GRATEFUL FOR THE MAJOR SUPPORT PROVIDED BY:

academy of american poets

THE PAUL G. ALLEN
FAMILY FOUNDATION

amazon *literary partnership*

POETRY FOUNDATION

4 CULTURE

Lannan

the point
envision·enact·evolve

ART WORKS. | National Endowment for the Arts
arts.gov

WASHINGTON STATE
ARTS COMMISSION

A&
OFFICE OF ARTS & CULTURE
SEATTLE

The Witter Bynner Foundation
for Poetry

TO LEARN MORE ABOUT UNDERWRITING
COPPER CANYON PRESS TITLES,
PLEASE CALL 360-385-4925 EXT. 103

WE ARE GRATEFUL FOR THE MAJOR SUPPORT PROVIDED BY:

Richard Andrews and
  Colleen Chartier
Anonymous
Jill Baker and Jeffrey Bishop
Anne and Geoffrey Barker
Donna Bellew
Will Blythe
John Branch
Diana Broze
John R. Cahill
Sarah Cavanaugh
Keith Cowan and Linda Walsh
Stephanie Ellis-Smith and
  Douglas Smith
Mimi Gardner Gates
Gull Industries Inc.
  on behalf of William True
William R. Hearst III
Carolyn and Robert Hedin
David and Jane Hibbard
Bruce S. Kahn
Phil Kovacevich and Eric Wechsler

Lakeside Industries Inc.
  on behalf of Jeanne Marie Lee
Maureen Lee and Mark Busto
Ellie Mathews and Carl Youngmann
  as The North Press
Larry Mawby and Lois Bahle
Hank and Liesel Meijer
Petunia Charitable Fund and
  adviser Elizabeth Hebert
Madelyn S. Pitts
Suzanne Rapp and Mark Hamilton
Adam and Lynn Rauch
Emily and Dan Raymond
Joseph C. Roberts
Cynthia Sears
Kim and Jeff Seely
D.D. Wigley
Barbara and Charles Wright
In honor of C.D. Wright,
  from Forrest Gander
Caleb Young as C. Young Creative
The dedicated interns and faithful
  volunteers of Copper Canyon Press

The pressmark for Copper Canyon Press
suggests entrance, connection, and interaction
while holding at its center
an attentive, dynamic space for poetry.

This book is set in Adobe Garamond Pro and LTC Goudy Oldstyle Pro.
Book design and composition by Becca Fox Design.
Printed on archival-quality paper.